"In this book of brilliantly linked poems, identity is information: the more of it we have, the more mysterious we become. 'Where will the deer sleep?' comes from the same place, and is given the same weight, as 'Why do we hope?' Is to weigh to lose, or to better define, yourself? We are made to forget what we bring to what we see. Full of calm and disorientation. Like saying the same word over and over until it loses meaning, but as though you were seeking that loss; as though, eyes wide, you can feel something, you know not what, has opened."

– Evan Karp, creator and director of Quiet Lightning

"Using minimalist language, visual imagery, humor and twists of logic, Maw Shein Win illuminates the single lens that sees the inner and the outer world at the same time. The first section, 'Score,' creates a compelling narrative of moments. The second section, 'Bone' creates a compelling narrative of experience; Maw Shein Win is a brilliant and stealthy guide. She brings to light the paradoxical nature of experience and will alter your vision of the world."

– Thaisa Frank, author of *Heidegger's Glasses* (2010) and *Enchantment* (2012)

"In *Score and Bone,* Maw Shein Win reduces narrative, perception, and memory to synecdoche and metonym; reality is posed as a problem of scale (macro- to microscopic perceiving and remembering) and movement from part to part, object to object. These deceptively simple, simply evocative, poems remind us that we humans, a part of the cultural and natural worlds, are all differently abled. And those differences are too a manifestation of the known and unknown universe."

– Tyrone Williams, author of *Red Between Green* (2015), *Howell* (2011), *On Spec* (2008), and other books

"In *Score and Bone*, Maw Shein Win's poems demonstrate a maturation of perspective, more considered risk taking, and a deepening of self-understanding. Written in a variety of free-verse forms, and largely in declarative, end-stopped lines (like film stills) that serve to modulate feeling and regulate the relentless tumble of images, Win's poems simultaneously contain and displace, fragment and cohere, illuminate and constrain ('Morning glories beautify and suffocate the pine tree'). The speaker's tone throughout is subdued, even dispassionate; feeling and story are conveyed obliquely via stark, stacked images ('The forest burns a violent red. Deer leap from the flames, singed flanks.'). A pervasive sense of dislocation is tempered by references to the body, to the material. Ranging across subjects that include the dissolution of a marriage, alienation, dream and fantasy, and hip surgery, *Score and Bone* is 'A hybrid, a mystery, a biopic' and represents Win's coming into her own brave and singular voice."

– Mari L'Esperance, author of *The Darkened Temple* (2008)

Score and Bone

Maw Shein Win

Nomadic Press
2016

This book was made possible by a loving community of family and friends, old and new.

Requests for permission to make copies of any part of the work should be sent to
info@nomadicpress.org.

For author questions or to book a reading at your school, bookstore, or alternative
establishment, please send an email to info@nomadicpress.org.

Published by Nomadic Press, 2926 Foothill Boulevard, Oakland, California, 94601
www.nomadicpress.org

First Edition
First Printing

Printed in the United States

Library of Congress Cataloging-in-Publication Data

Win, Maw Shein, 1963 –
Score and Bone/written by Maw Shein Win; illustrated by Arthur Johnstone and Livien Yin
p. cm.
Summary: Via two alternating voices—interior (observed) and narrative (observer)—that
speak to one another, the striking, image-rich poems in *Score and Bone*'s two sections
delve into the subjects of film and perception, body and memory, and lead the reader
through a visceral cinematic landscape.
[1. POETRY / Subjects & Themes / Film 2. POETRY / Subjects & Themes / Health. 3.
POETRY / American / General.] I. Title.

2016953754

ISBN: 978-0-9970933-7-7

The illustrations in this book were created using pen and marker on Canson paper.
The type was set in Garamond Premier Pro.
Printed and bound in the United States
Typesetting and book design by J. K. Fowler
Edited by Arisa White and J. K. Fowler

for

Thomas Salvatore Scandura

CONTENTS

BONE

SCORE

SCORE

The film score is a Turkish bathhouse, a thankless accountant, a back-country road in Montana, a shy teenager, a wine glass with a painting of a cow on it, the underbelly of a cat, the stream running along the outside of a prison, the shadow of an orchid, a heroin addict, a blanket statement, a lemon rolling down the hill, a blister on the tip of a finger, a forest ranger, a chunk of ice melting, a bully, a bowl of fresh honey, an abandoned baby, two bank robbers drinking coffee, the edge of the volcano, a loose belt, a sorrowful laugh, a broad brushstroke, three dice, the left side of his face, and an orange coat left on a park bench. The blue light hitting the Venetian glass in a way that the heroine could only imagine.

FILM #1

You have holes in your energy field.
The therapist announced.
The husband was dismayed.
His wife brought her hand to her mouth.
Your holes need to be filled.
This will be the focus of our next three sessions.
Close-up of the therapist's face.
Eyes closed. Glass teardrop on her upper cheek.

FILM #2

A young woman walks on crutches towards a garden.
She wears a long cape that trails behind her.
A boy stands alongside the dirt road and offers her strawberries.
A man on a donkey pulls an empty wooden cart.
Close-up of the woman's feet.
Frayed leather sandals. A star-shaped birthmark on her left ankle.
A metaphor. Or a sign.

FILM #3

He is a self-proclaimed healer from Holland.
He believes that people who are ill can be cured by submerging
their bodies in ice-cold water.
Men leap off cliffs into ice lakes in the winter.
Men sit naked in the forest up to their shoulders in snow.
The first thing he says to her: *You radiate pure love energy.*
And then, *You are unaware of your power over those around you.*
He finishes his beer and pops open another one with his teeth.
Close-up of an ice cube slowly melting on her tongue.

CLOSE-UPS

Two boys sit on a log in the middle of a valley. The trees surrounding them block out the sunlight and the boys have trouble seeing their hands in front of their faces. A woman appears from a cluster of trees. She holds a basket in one hand and a jug of water in the other. Her eyes are closed and she walks towards them as if she can see. She can, in fact, see through her eyelids. The boys are entranced by her silver hair and wonder what is in the basket. They stretch their hands out towards her.

FILM #4

Where should we meet in our dreams? he asks.
In Greece, on a beach, at dusk, she replies. And then, *Do you need more earplugs?*
She counts, *One thousand, two thousand, three thousand.*
He is asleep. A deep and heavy snore.
Long shot of industrial landscape.

FILM #5

She uncorks a bottle of Cabernet at 4:30 pm.
A slight buzzing in her ears. Pleasing.
A sliver of pain through her left thigh. Remote.
She thinks about her ex. He used to live here and his shoes were over there.
The landlord sends a text. She doesn't respond.
She lifts the glass to her lips. Close up of her teeth. Crooked on the top row.

Straight on the bottom.

The sound of the fridge. Chilling.
Long shot of a woman as she slowly walks to the radio and turns it on.

The voice of the radio announcer: *Never mind the fog alert, ladies and gents. A calf will be born in the morning. Buy everything before you forget. The song that you just heard was by.*

More vision for all!

SIX SHORT FILMS

1

Long shot of shins wrapped in cotton gauze.
Red maple tree outside the window and below the balcony.
A bowl of lemons on the neighbor's porch.

2

A blindfold wound around a man's bleeding head.
Wide angle view of a playground, children playing kickball in the dirt.
Hummingbirds captured in soft light.

3

The ending starts at the beginning.
Sound of a couple arguing in a restaurant.
Or the other way around.

4

Her pupils of soft brazen green.
Many bees escaped from the colony.
A murder mystery for a limited audience.

5

The soft tissue under his armpits.
Laughter in the bedroom.
An abandoned farm and a deserted mall.

6

Hand-held camera scenes of a college reunion.
A chronicle of one woman's journey through Tibet.
The factory workers assembling toy soldiers and ballerinas.

FILM #7

In the opening sequence, the train pulls into the station.
It is 7:00 am, overcast.

Black-and-white palette.
The light is dim and the sky is dim.

A woman in a black coat steps off the platform of the train.
Close-up of her partially closed eyes.

A white cat darts through the legs of the crowd jostling towards the exit.
A boy clutching a burlap bag falls down and four apples roll out.
No one looks.

Zoom in on the conductor pulling a cord above his head.
A sharp whistling sound.
Extreme close-up of the boy's hand grabbing one of the fallen apples.

FILM #8

The story line does not have an element of suspense or terror.
The story is about a woman who wants to find her missing brother.
Her father had an extramarital affair when she was three years old.

All these years I have wanted to tell you that you have a brother about your age.
You won't be able to find him. His name is John and he looks like you.

Sound of raindrops hitting the porch.
Someone trying to start a car.
Close-up of the brother's eyes, dark and unforgiving.

MEDIUM SHOT

A tall woman and a small man walk down the street one late morning in a town in New Hampshire. They look confused and weathered and people stare at them as they pass by. She picks up a coin on the street and holds it up in the light to examine the year. He grabs the coin from her hand and tosses it in the trashcan. She continues to walk then stops to admire some roses in someone's garden. He sticks his face into the flowers. She counts three drops of blood and a few petals on the glittering sidewalk.

FILM #9

Opening shot: a phone booth on the corner of an empty parking lot.
Drizzling rain.
A man holds a wet rolled-up newspaper.
The telephone rings.
The man picks up the receiver.
His ear is sweaty and his coat is wet.
He hears the voice of a woman.
She sounds far away.
He stutters, then coughs, then hangs up.

Connections in the telephone booth.
Crossed connections.
Crossed eyes. Shut then open. Then shut again.
Cross country.

On the street:
A briefcase
A cake box
A plastic sandal
A quarter

Cross over to the other side.
Across bridges and roads and sidewalks.
The man looks up and through and beyond the glass.

FILM #10

She's sitting in a café in downtown Oakland.
It's the middle of the day.

Flashback: she is an x-ray technician.
Guiding the patients in blue cotton robes to the table.

Moving their limbs under the projections, calming words.
Third cup of coffee and half a bagel on a cracked plate.

She looks at the young man sitting at a table next to her.
Long moustache and expensive brown shoes.

Close-up of his eyes blinking rapidly. The screen goes dark.

SHORTS

The auteur has run out of pain pills. Panic.

A hybrid, a mystery, a biopic.

Space is an oddity some believe.

Extreme close up of bright orange peel on wooden floor.

A crow hops its way closer to the electric gate.

Smokestacks on the horizon.

My teeth are covered with guilt.

And sometimes beauty.

DIALOGUES #12

I recognize her voice because it's my voice. I don't know that name because it's his name. You thought you heard my voice, but it was your voice. I think your voice has a name, but it's my name.

She met herself in a restaurant. It wasn't her restaurant, but it was a place she had been before. She had eaten eggs there. Potatoes Anna. The dishes had no names. But the waiter had a high voice.

How could you not remember me? We were married last May.

The cakes were baked by professionals. One of them looked like a marvelous dress.

What will you bring to the table? What is your sir, name?
What are the camels doing here?

Please. Change. For. Me.

Are those your wind chimes?

RANDOM FILMS SHOTS #15

1

A Brownie camera slung around her sweaty neck.

A wooden totem pole on the edge of the cliff.

California poppies crushed by dark army boots.

2

Telephone wires crisscross.
You didn't hear that, did you?
You did, now, didn't you?

A child in a blue cape leaps through the garden.

Three wild hogs and a mild cat.

3

Black-and-white self-portraits in bathroom mirrors and bakery windows.

The sun burns the skin off the forehead.

History has had its way.

TWO DOCUMENTARIES

1

Where will the deer sleep? I thought about this last night as I always do.

Why do we hope? *Hope and beauty are obsolete constructs*, she wrote, *useless for women.*

How does a painting speak? Language is the difference among three things.

Who enters the diorama? The brave ones with their silk ties.

2

The dining room table was set for six. One missing spoon.

My neighbor captures escaped bees with a butterfly net.

The forest burns a violent red. Deer leap from the flames, singed flanks.

Hold on now to what's left.

THE TREACHERY OF IMAGES

The sun is a cymbal.
A cat is a bear.
An accordion is a frosted cupcake.

A gargoyle is a steering wheel.
The barber is a valley.
A tulip is a black-and-white film.

Architecture is a mustard sandwich.
A wild turkey is a forest.
The director is a fur sweater.

A mansion is a savage gown.
The guard is catnip.
A mink is a caveat.

The pipe is a magnolia tree.

The magnolia tree is a blanket. The blanket is a flamingo. The flamingo is
a beach mat. The beach mat is a soldier. The soldier is a tangerine.
The tangerine is a villa. The villa is a pony. The pony is a peony growing
from a crack in the driveway of an abandoned tool shed.

THE MISSING

1

A river of damp green runs through the burnt orange valley.

The swimmers in the diamond-shaped lake at night.

The trees burst open, petals landing on cotton dresses.

The children have disappeared! Parents weep in empty homes.

2

A chalkboard. A basket of fresh berries. Lost signals.

The opera singer brings tears to their eyes.

The swimmers near the lake. Shivering.

A painting in the studio. Glittering.

3

The television doesn't work anymore. Nor does the oven.

The deer have gone the wrong direction. *Turn around and head for the hills.*

The painter tracks green house paint on the blank canvas.

The girls were in school to learn. Their packed lunches in satchels.

4

Mother cuts the melon into sections and puts them on chipped plates.

She calls out, *The fruit is ready. Come home now!*

Streaks of teal and vermillion. Layers upon layers.

The deer can't find their way back to the hills.

BONE

UNDER TONES

The eye is seldom there
Nor is a chair

Tiny tendrils of hair
A single and extended tone

Under the box is
The story of a bone

THE WHEELCHAIR

The scar is a girl and the wheelchair is a woman. The crutch is butch. The drugs are good. The light is dry. The air is paint. The bed isn't there. The nurse wears a cape and the doctor is a child. The wheelchair is there. The scar is at a loss. The wheel catches light off the reflection of water in a bag. The bag is on a pole. The walker is a technician in blue pants. The scar cream isn't there. The air is blue paint. The light is a small boy with his face in the pillow. The crutch is a doctor with a diamond on her forehead. The diamond is a tunnel with a one-way road. The ambulance drives towards the east. The bed is dry paint and the scar rejects the water. The boy is there and the bag trickles tiny blue diamonds.

THE THERMOMETER

The numbers have meaning. The red line. The black lines. The tongue pale pink with deep rivers. Temperature low. The bruise on the shin. Signs of people who lived there. The children who played on the shin. The red river. The black numbers. The pink bruise. The thermometer underneath the bed. Beyond the bed, there lived a village. The signs of people who died there. An undetermined number. The temperature has meaning. A child slipped on his shin into the pink river. She landed on a cabbage leaf and floated toward the blinking red lights of the blue city.

THE CANE

She balances the cane on her right foot. Spins like a dancer. The cane reaches out to him. Bright log. A rice cracker on the floor. A sliver of dark chocolate and ginger. A chisel of pain through the knee. Do not cross the ankles. Do not bend over. Do not swivel at the waist. She uses her elbows to reach out to him. The dancer rotates at 90 degrees. The cane is a bent poppy. The cane is a dancer in the recovery room bending over and looking at the cracker broken on the floor. The orange is ravishing.

THE PHYSICAL THERAPIST

Her name is June. She stands up straight. Her legs are strong. She wears a red sweater with bright green jewels sewn on. Her hair is white. She answers my long questions with short answers.

She was thrown from a horse when she was 27 and ended up in a wheelchair unable to walk. She slept through the surgery and dreamt about wild deer in a dark forest.

My left foot drags across the wood floor as my right leg moves the weight of my body forward. Chromium and ceramic parts in the hip. I rub sesame oil on my joints at night. I take another pill.

June visits on Tuesdays and Thursdays. I listen for the sound of her car in the driveway. I lift my legs up and off the wheelchair and onto the floor. My skin is a dry lakebed, cracked and unremarkable. I look at the peeling red paint on my toenails. Feet I cannot touch.

She checks my blood pressure and takes my temperature. Pain is measured on a scale of one to ten. I say, *seven, no eight*. She pushes up her sleeves and stands in the kitchen next to the sink. She slowly swings her muscular left leg behind her. *Like this,* she says. *Not that.*

When I was 18, I slipped off the saddle of a horse, my body dangling from the side of its hard long flanks. I counted to ten and pulled my body upwards. The leather of the saddle cutting into my palms. The horse, calm and unmoving.

THE DRESSING STICK

The dressing stick, a limb
on the edge of the green
and a twinkling star on the head
of a small bear, polydactyl paws,
matted skin, a seven-inch scar on the left hip.

She peeled the scar back and underneath found a child wearing a star hat
and star shoes. The hospital stood in the center of a large cornfield and
observers remarked at its beauty and precision.

They came bearing frankincense and Oxycontin.
They wore shields.
They could sew.

They came bearing pork and beef on platters.
They held liquid in wires.

She waved the dressing stick and the wires spelled words to her
through the window of the blue tent.

THE OPERATED LEG

Isolate the pain, the size of a buffalo nickel. Draw a circle around it.

Lift top half of torso onto elbows. Rest. Move right leg first, then left.
Slow, then methodical.

A car alarm goes off down the street. A medicine bottle falls off the nightstand
and rolls under the bed.

The cat folds her head deeper into sleep.

With left foot, pull walker towards mattress. Lift knee. Rest.

The pain is a bright coin in the middle of the street.
Taxis and motorcycles speed by.

Stop. Focus on the sensation of gravity pulling feet to floorboard. Look for
doorknob and pull open.

Stare into eye of the scar.

THE GRABBER

A river of rock, drop, lets off pain by the side,
a long scar on the side of the code,
chickens crossing, here and where.

Why, why,
the laughter inside the fist of the grabber,
an extension
of arm reaching out
to platters, of eggs and jam.

A village of medicine bottles,
amber and blue.
She runs on four legs along the dry
river, bed, her mother, sleeping.

She continues to run, the sun, blinking.

The scar, a question mark.

Why, why the chickens

Why, why jam and eggs

Why, why the handful of grabbers

Bottles of joy-laughter.

OBJECTS

A blue glass bowl of miniature oranges.
Three inches from arm's reach.

I eye objects in terms of distance now.
Reachable. Then not.

This morning I drop a plastic tub
of butter on the kitchen floor.

I try to reach it with my grabber. The lid slides off.
The butter tips and my cat starts to lick.

The objects in my life with more significance:
wheelchair over umbrella. Walker over work shoes. Bed tray over sunglasses.

I measure distance from hand to knee to shin to heel.
I think of Burma, miles away. The grocery store, miles away.

My father's voice crackles through the phone, miles and miles away.
He: *You were born in Burma.* And then, *You're my niece, right?*

I push my body upwards from my wheelchair.
I know that above the ceiling are wood and plaster and eventually sky and birds.

Objects, found and lost: my ex-husband's brown sandals, loose feathers from a
bird that my cat killed, a large, smooth seed given to me by the owner of a flower
shop in Tokyo.

I look down at the floor trying to remember.

THE OTHER NIGHT

Protrusio acetabuli: an uncommon condition of the bones.
The specialist warns of breakage, complications on the table.

Somewhere a red-tailed hawk. Palm leaves about to fall.
A young man running up a stairwell. She is in the *Bauhaus Room*.

Remnants from former inhabitants in the desk drawer: blackened
candle wicks, coins from Poland. The ilium, the ischium, the pubis.

The protrusio may progress until the femoral neck impinges against the pelvis.
A condition to be accepted or defied.

A rumor that the house is haunted. Outside the leaves lie on the ground.
Morning glories beautify and suffocate the pine tree.

Traces of every person loved or unloved held in her hips.

FIVE DAYS IN A CITY

The houseplant moved on its own volition across the planked floor.
Trails of laughing beetles.
An eye. An egg. A riverbed.

Twins growing in the belly of her niece.
Imprint. Cyclic.
Ginkgo leaves spilling from trees
in front of brick facades.

The grandmother adorned in costume jewelry sips
from a flask of brandy in the morning.
The mother holds her arm up high,

an unlit match in her hand.
Broken, she tells her children. *Your arms are broken, too.*
We're going to the hospital.

Sunken cheeks of models, tiny birds fallen out of nests.
A paper boat adrift on a lake. She considers forgiveness.
A man on crutches curses the lack of elevators in the subway station.

Six maple trees and a flattened starflower in a silver frame.

MOUNTAIN

The bruise around the scar is magenta.
A majesty of magenta.
The magenta of frosted teacakes in Switzerland.
Magenta of pain and suffering.
Majesty of sugar and joy.

The scar is a mountain.
Hike the frosted peaks in the Alps.
Children high on sugar peeking through the trees.
Fingertips in the frosting.
Magenta-colored bruises.

Mercury is a state of mind.
A planet for children where frosted teacakes grow on trees.
Majesty of pain.
Children running, running
on a sugar high to the top of the magenta mountain.

THINGS THAT BEGIN

1

Tinctures for sparrow. Capsized pumpkin. Shadow blots. *Memento mori.*
Ladder to sky. Dreaming crickets. Elephant key.
Contained custards. Braided turnips.
Tempests and gladiators.
Painted things.

2

Riotous hips and ribcage. A being-filled with liquid. *Stop, stop now.*
Please, continue. Over is it yet?
The doctor's eyelashes are butterflies. She was a little man. He was a little woman.
Sleeping children with locks and tresses. Lost in the desert. Found in the forest.
Pointed things.

3

Crushed tundra and crossed eyes. Trinkets and sceptres and waterfalls in Brazil.
He believes in magic and so do I. Dragon fruit scooped into bowls.
Owls and blue spaces in sparkling lots. Matters can complicate matters.
A slithering towards.
Planted things.

ARE YOU IN THE ROOM WITH ME NOW?

My therapist asked why I never cry.
I ask myself the same, closing my eyes.
A small sty in my vision.

As hard as I tried not to cry,
I was shy as a child. As I crossed the street
with mother, I hid behind her lab coat.

My throat taut and tight.
I thought I might cry.
The other night I lost my sight.

I could hear a couple on the crosswalk.
A man doing a handstand.
Two kids making plans.

Perhaps a chance to dance
in another place. I could cross the state
line. Cry at the sight of a shimmering lake.

My therapist asked:
What are you thinking? How does that make you feel?
Where did that come from
and are you in the room with me now?

In Rio, there is a majestic cross on a cliff.
People live in pink paper shacks below.
I danced and I drank there.
I thought I might die there.
I crossed myself although I didn't believe.

You sweat silver tears.
You see through pink paper walls.
You think your body might be crying now.

ACKNOWLEDGEMENTS

Many thanks to the editors of the following journals in which some of these poems have appeared, sometimes in slightly different versions: *Zócalo Public Square, vitriol, The Fabulist, Eleven Eleven, Ping Pong Literary Journal, Apasiology, Moonshine Baby, Cimarron Review, Up the Staircase Quarterly, Babel Fruit, Big Bridge, Fanzine,* and *The Careless Embrace of the Boneshaker,* an anthology by great weather for MEDIA. Grateful to Neeli Cherkovski and Bill Mohr, editors of *Cross-Strokes, an Anthology of Los Angeles and San Francisco Poetry,* for including my work.

Most of the poems in this collection were written during my recovery period following my hip replacement surgeries. I am forever grateful to my dear friends and family who helped out in so many ways: visits, meals, letters, and writing dates. Special thanks to my sister, Thet, who organized my dream team and for all of her support.

My deepest gratitude to publisher J. K. Fowler for believing in my work and for being such a strong supporter of writers, as well as to editor Arisa White, MK Chavez, Paul Corman-Roberts, and the rest of the Nomadic Press family.

My heartfelt thanks to Thaisa Frank, Judy Halebsky, Joyce Jenkins, Evan Karp, Mari L'Esperance, and Tyrone Williams for their beautiful and thoughtful blurbs.

Many thanks to my lovely friends and fellow writers and artists, Jenny Bitner, Mary and Hugh Behm-Steinberg, Yvonne Campbell, Amanda Chaudhary, Sharon Coleman, Tim Donnelly, Jack Foley, Steve Gilmartin, Lael Gold, Annice Jacoby, Patricia Kelly, Vince Montague, Peggy Morrison, Kathleen Munnelly, Annabelle Port, Cybele Zufolo Siegel, Susan Smyth, Christopher Statton, Amos White, and Megan Wilson. Thank you, Kelsey.

Much gratitude to the members of my two amazing writing groups: Lea Aschkenas, Laurie Kirkpatrick, Kara Knafelc, Margaret Stawowy; and Heather Bourbeau, Chris Cook, Kathleen McClung, Amanda Williamsen, and Josh Wilson.

I would like to thank my best friends, Adrian de la Peña and Mark Dutcher, who have supported me with their friendship and creative inspiration for over 30 years. I could not have done this book without them. Finally, my love and gratitude to my partner in time, Thomas Scandura, to whom this book is dedicated.

My sincerest apologies to anyone I may have overlooked. I thank you.

MAW SHEIN WIN is a Burmese American poet, editor, and educator who lives and works in the Bay Area. Her writing has appeared in many print and online journals and most recently in the anthology *Cross-Strokes: Poetry Between Los Angeles and San Francisco* (Otis Books/Seismicity Editions). *Ruins of a glittering palace*, her collaborative chapbook, with paintings by Mark Dutcher, was published by SPA/Commonwealth Projects. She is a poetry editor for *Rivet: The Journal of Writing that Risks* and was selected as the first poet laureate of El Cerrito, California.